AFRICA
The Land of Dreams

EDRIS KIBALAMA

ISBN:9798775698065

"...finding a new spiritual algorithm that would allow me to live positively, safely and peacefully on all levels in Nigeria- by the will of Allah"- Edris Kibalama

CONTENTS

Table of Contents

INTRODUCTION

Bismillah Arrahman Arraheem

In the name of Allah, The Entirely Merciful,

The Especially Merciful

Alhamdulillah/All praise be to Allah

The Salah and salaam on the Final Messenger

of Allah(Muhammad peace of Allah be upon

him)

To proceed:

This is a book that I compiled from a deep personal experience with my fellow African family, of which I was impacted spiritually. I had to make sense of my new environment, and adjust myself (as in- finding a new spiritual algorithm that would allow me to live positively, safely and peacefully on all levels in Africa- by the will of Allah

May Allah guide us all Ameen
May Allah forgive me my sins and May He pardon my mistakes

Alhamdulillah/All praise be to Allah

The Salah and salaam on the Final Messenger of Allah(Muhammad peace of Allah be upon him)

Edris Kibalama

Rabi Thaani 1443 AH

THE TEXT

AFRICA- The land of dreams

Africa is truly a land of attaining your wildest dreams as far as this temporary world is considered.

I have experienced lots of challenges, but my Creator, Allah subhaana wa ta 'aala has made the situation much more clearer to me in relation to the whole black/ African slavery and the so called colonialism of the Western Powers(for lack of a better term)

Just in-case you did not know, most of the academic books available, for example, in the Kaduna metropolis area; the majority of these books are outdated, many of them even being books from the 1980's/199i0's and possibly even before.

As it is said, you can not judge a person until you walk a thousand mile/steps in their shoes. So, having generally analyzed the situation in the bookshops in Kaduna Metropolis, in general, as stated above, most of the books are second hand, which in and of itself sends a bold message to the intellectual African man of both past and present that the Western world has spent almost endless resources, time, effort, finances(mostly taken from the so-called colonized lands- we may come back to this particular conundrum at a later point) and deliberate mis-information about the African man of both past and present i.e. black Africa's rich heritage of wealth, natural resources and moreso, multitudes of fully orgamized, self- governing Kingdoms etc spread across black Africa.

I will be at the foremost at affirming that; I do not have a general problem with anyone in this world with regards to geneaology parse. However having said that, I do not believe that this lack of looking down on other nations(albeit being correct both from the natural disposition and divine law), should give way to Arab/ Asian/ White supremacy to take charge.

I personally have no general problem with regards to different nations such as the British, Italians, French coming to our lands to share and trade in the resources that Allah provided to his creation, and the Arabs coming through the so-called horn of Africa, East Africa and through most of North Africa to trade, and most especially spread Islam (to the point where there are several lands in black Africa that are majority muslim). However, this does not justify a non- legislated reverence of a particular genealogy, moreso to the point of worshiping the Creation(the worst sin that Allah does not forgive if repentance is not ardently and sincerely sought before the time of one's death)

Trading resources, whether locally or globally(as related to my point above) does not justify cheating, deception, financial/ social/ racial/ economic subjugation without a permission from divine law, let alone demoralisation, perpetual ridicule on all levels(including physical, mental, spiritual and intellectual) of a group of people with the only justification being an action directly inherited from Iblees himself(the sin he not only committed but also persisted in, to the point where he refused to repent to Allah)

Adam and Hawa(peace be upon them) sought and received forgiveness, guidance and positive respite from The Creator)

However, Iblees, did not repent and furthermore made the oaths he made to Allah(His Lord as he himself testified by his asking of His Rabb to give him respite and experiencing his Creator disfiguring him, eternally cursing him and promising him the fire of hell as an eternal abode). So to keep this particular point short, if this is the type of inheritance you wish for, then this book is not necessarily for you, wa Allahu a'lam

Contarary to common and deliberate mis-information (for whatever reason), many people across the world do not realise that there exists in the Arab lands, dark skin Arab tribes, even from the times of Prophet Muhammad(and even before).

Hajar, the Mother of Ismael and the wife of Ibrahim(peace be upon them all) was a dark skinned/ black individual, from what is known to the best of my recall. So from well known understanding of geneaology by its experts, some of the traits/ characteristics of a particular ancestor is highly likely (to say the least), to reach down to any number of generations which Our Creator has decreed.

This difference in complexions/ characteristics of some of the Prophets is testified to in the famous book Shamail Attirmidhi, in which Imam Tirmidhi(Rahimuhullah) compiles the explanations of the difference in complexion between Prophet Muusa(peace upon him),

Prophet Ibrahim(Peace be upon him) and

Prophet Muhammad(peace be upon him)

It is clear to those with sound intellect and a

pure heart that there is obviously a Wisdom

of Allah Subhaana wa ta 'Aala that those who

are well known (in Orthodox Islam), to be the

three greatest Prophet's, had the differences in

their complexions described to us.

Also, these three Prophets were amongst those

that Allah took as his Khaleel, and those that

Allah spoke to directly. Those who understand

this wisdom, Alhmadulillah, and those that

don't, we pray that Allah makes us better than

they think, May Allah increase us in beneficial knowledge. May Allah guide us, May Allah forgive us all our sins, and we ask Allah that he pardons us our shortcomings. May Allah purify our hearts and intentions, May Allah give us understanding of the religion, May Allah give us beneficial knowledge, hikmah and sincerity for His sake Alone. May Allah have Mercy and forgiveness upon us and those who preceeded us.

Oh Allah guide us all Ameen

Rabbanaa, Aatinaa fiddunia hasanah, wa fil akhirati hasanah, wa qinaa 'adhabannaar

Alhamdulillah, wassalatu wassalaam 'alaa

Rasuulillah

Translation:

Our Lord/ Rabb, Give us the good of this

world and give us the good of the afterlife and

protect us from the fire of Hell Ameen

All praises belong to Allah, and the salah and

the salaam upon the final

Messenger(Muhammad Peace be upon him)

FINAL PRAYER

All Praises abundant and plentiful belong to Allah, and peace be upon his final Messenger Muhammad, peace and blessings be upon him, his family, his companions and all of those that follow them till the day of Judgement.

FINAL WORD

If you liked the reflective quotes, check out in the links below what was part of the fruits of this work:

1. www.edriskibalama.com

A website on creatively designed inspirational quotes images and a portfolio section outlining my achievements thus far.

2. www.muslimhomeschoolsoftware.com

A website on Home Educational Software for children with an Islamised and Ethical curriculum

3. www.intelligentmindsconsultancy.com

A website on IT support, WordPress support and IT consultancy

4. www.eddykibs.com

More of my inspirational quotes merchandise

5. To contact me and see my works:

www.linkedin.com/in/edriskibalama/

6. Other published books

Search: "Edris Kibalama" on

<u>www.amazon.co.uk</u>

BONUS CHAPTER 1

Extracts taken from:

Reflections of an Orthodox Islamic Immigrant

1. Parable of the importance of knowledge:

Know your button mushroom from a magic

mushroom, as eating one is a blessing, and eating the other is a potential sin.

2. Parable on dedication: When the light refuses to switch on, use an alternative power supply.

3. Importance of travel: Sometimes, the things you wish for are not always in the locality you currently reside in.

4. Tests of Allah: It is not until you live deeply amongst the ignorant , that you would know whether you are yourself the same.

5. In a land of deep seated Jahiliyyah, I give you an advice my fellow brother or sister, never open Pandora's box even if you can physically get out eventually, the spiritual, emotional and intellectual damage to your being may never heal.

Important lesson; Never argue with an ignorant one. Don't even contemplate or think about it.

6. Always turn back to the Creator. Don't let the people's negative, abusive and derogatory words put you down. Trust in Allah, He will

fulfill his promise to those who fear and trust

Him alone.

7. If you are following a path that you are not

meant to follow, the Creator will make it very

clear to you, as long as you constantly seek

His counsel. (i.e. Istikhaarah), you are sincere

and you demonstrate never-ending patience

(only for the sake of Allah)

BONUS CHAPTER 2

Statements on the reality of Orthodox Islamic Zuhd

1. Most poor people are not actually Zuhaad.

2. The richest man can be the greatest Zaahid than the poorest of people

3. Zuhd is a state of heart not necessarily a state of physical existence.

4. If most people knew the status of a true Zaahid (i.e. those that died in the pleasure of

Allah) no one on this earth would dare to even utter a word of negativity towards them, and moreover their Creator.

5. The Zuhaad are amongst the ones that Allah chooses to be from amongst His Awliyaa and from amongst His Khaleel

6. You'd rather abuse a mushrik than even attempt to have bad intentions towards a khaleel/ walii/ sincere a'rifun/ Zaahid of Allah

7. All the Prophets were Zuhaad

...This is a book that I compiled fro
a deep personal experience with r
fellow African fam...ity, of which I
was impacted spiritualy. I had to
make sense of my new
environment, and adjust myself (a
in- finding a new spiritual algorith
that would allow me to live
positively, safely and peacefully or
all levels in Africa- by the will of
Allah...

May Allah guide us all Ameen

La cortesía

Hilda M. Gutiérrez
de Alvarado